The Consumers' Guide To Long Term Care Insurance

By

Stephen F. Rowley

ISBN: 1-4140-3868-2 (e-book)
ISBN: 1-4140-3867-4 (Paperback)

Library of Congress Control Number: 2003098775

This book is printed on acid free paper.

Printed in the United States of America
Bloomington, IN

1stBooks - rev. 01/16/04

Dedicated to my Mother and Father

May their retirement years be filled with health, happiness, and independence!

About The Author

The author is uniquely qualified to address the important issues of Long Term Care insurance. As Vice President of Risk Management for a major international reinsurer he works closely with countless insurers and consulting firms. His responsibilities include oversight of both underwriting and claims management processes. He has supervised the development of comprehensive risk management guides that have become standards in the Long Term Care industry. The author's responsibilities in the reinsurance market provide him with an extremely broad perspective of industry practices. In addition to his underwriting and claims duties, he is involved in the analysis of insurance policies, contract language, and pricing discussions.

With more than fifteen years of insurance experience, the author is a well-recognized and respected leader of the Long Term Care insurance industry. He is active in numerous industry events and conferences. He is a founding member, and past president, of the Long Term Care International Forum. He has worked closely with the Society of Actuaries on Long Term Care education and is a frequent speaker at industry events.

Above all, the author is someone who believes in the value and importance of Long Term Care insurance and has advocated responsible stewardship of the public trust. He has had the pleasure of working with the brightest and most creative people in the industry and has used that experience in this book to demystify Long Term Care insurance.

Table of Contents

Introduction

"Wish not so much to live long
as to live well."

Benjamin Franklin

Insurance today is developed using a highly complex group of mathematical equations. At its roots, however, is a simple and easy to understand philosophy. The fundamental principle of insurance is to spread the risk of loss over a significant number of individuals so that each person pays a small premium in order to ensure that they will never have to suffer a catastrophic financial loss.

Long Term Care (LTC) insurance does this by collecting regular premiums in return for promising to pay all or part of the cost of the insureds Long Term Care expenses should they ever require it. Long Term Care expenses may include payments to nursing homes, assisted living facilities, or for care provided in ones home.

Long Term Care insurance is among the youngest of all insurance products. In many ways, the Long Term Care industry has just left its infancy and is heading into the toddler years. These developmental years will be marked by growth, exploration and more than a few falls. Eventually, we will begin to see how the mature insurance product will look and behave.

In the meantime, like all toddlers, the LTC industry is bound to make mistakes, throw a few tantrums, and behave in ways that will embarrass its more mature insurance cousins. Likewise, the talented, innovative minds leading the LTC industry today will no doubt become the envy of the market as they strive to develop products that our aging population and strained government resources so desperately need.

Like all insurance products, LTC will be more inclined to mature properly, and with fewer growing pains, under the watchful eye and guidance of the consumer. Only when the consumer truly understands the benefits and costs associated with Long Term Care protection will the industry be able to claim full maturity.

Purchasing a Long Term Care policy is an expensive, usually lifelong, decision. Once they purchase coverage, very few individuals allow it to lapse or replace it with a newer policy. The consumer's relationship with the insurer may span 20, 30, or even 40 years. Some of these years will be as a healthy premium payer, while others may be as a beneficiary.

For this reason, the consumer should take the time to fully understand the product that he or she purchases. It is equally important to determine the strength and stability of the insurance company providing the coverage.

This book is a guide to help you, the consumer, better understand Long Term Care insurance. The goal is to translate industry jargon and legalistic policy language into laymen's terms to help the purchasing public better understand the types of policies and features available in Long Term Care policies so that consumers can assess the value and limitations of Long Term Care insurance.

The following pages will help the consumer better comprehend the issues surrounding the need for Long Term Care as well as the types of policies and features available. This book should not be viewed as a recommendation or endorsement of any particular insurer or type of Long Term Care product. Each individual should determine his or her own needs and select the policy that best fulfills those needs.

<u>Aging</u>

*"If you live to the age of 100 you have it
made because very few people die
past the age of a hundred"*

George Burns

The 20th Century was the most remarkable in the history of mankind for improvement in life expectancy. The average life expectancy of a child born in the year 1900 was only 48 years. A child born today can expect to live an average of nearly 77 years. Life expectancy improved by an unprecedented 10 years between 1900 and 1930 alone and has continued to increase ever since.

This 29-year increase in average life expectancy during the 20th Century was primarily due to improvements in sanitation and health care. These improvements greatly diminished mortality among infants and young children. Diseases such as measles and polio, which once claimed thousands of young lives, were all but eliminated through routine childhood vaccinations. Loving parents who once lived in fear of diphtheria, scarlet fever, and smallpox soon took comfort in knowing that their children were protected against these devastating diseases.

However, not all of the improvements in life expectancy during the 20th Century were for children. Adults of all ages began to see an improved quality and quantity of life as unprecedented advances in health education, medicine, and technology began to emerge. These gains were augmented by new legislation designed to protect industrial workers, control pollution and air quality, and aid elderly citizens who could not afford appropriate health care in their later years.

When combined, these factors led to an impressive improvement in both the quality and quantity of life. A 65-year-old living in the year 2000 could expect to live 50 percent longer than a person who was 65 in the year 1900. Tremendous advantages in technology have been a significant factor in accelerating these results in the latter half of the century. Whereas the average remaining life expectancy of a 65-year-old improved 2.4 years in the first sixty years of the twentieth century, the nation saw an astounding 3.7 year increase during the remaining forty years.

Improvements in both child mortality rates and adult health paved the way for the "baby boomers", born in the 19 years following the end of World War II, to live the healthiest and most productive lives in the history of civilization. The United States today enjoys an estimated 35 million seniors over the age of 65. This number is expected to double to more than 70 million by the year 2030 when the last of the baby boomers turn 65.

Even more impressive are the number of centenarians, those who have reached the age of 100 or greater, living in our society today. Most estimates place this number at around 65,000. While that number is impressive, it will increase nearly six fold by the year 2030 to 381,000. By 2050, the number of centenarians may well exceed one million.

Although increased longevity is welcome news, there are many personal and societal challenges that accompany it. Everyone dreams of a long, happy and healthy life. Today's senior citizens have embraced a life longer than any could have imagined. Relatively few, however, have accepted or addressed the reality that their ability to function independently may be seriously compromised as they age. This is of tremendous concern given that nearly one half of all Americans over the age of 75 suffer some limitations caused by chronic disabilities.

With increasing age, chronic and debilitating illnesses may drastically change the quality of life. The ability to care for oneself may be challenged by both physical and cognitive deterioration. Many will be forced to rely on their family, friends, paid care providers, or government programs for care as they age. Few will be prepared for the financial and emotional burden that will be imposed on them and their loved ones should they lose the ability to care for themselves.

Such losses are a natural part of the aging process. Many seniors who experience diminished cognitive or physical abilities feel embarrassed or ashamed. They castigate themselves for losses that are a natural part of the aging process. The negative self-image suffered by many seniors is exacerbated by a lack of access to competent or humane care.

History and Evolution of Elder Care

*"Sure I'm for helping the elderly.
I'm going to be old myself some day"*

Lillian Carter, in her 80's

The task of caring for those who cannot care for themselves is a difficult one. Throughout most of history, and in most societies, the family has taken responsibility for the care of ailing and disabled family members who were unable to care for themselves. It was not unusual for a home to house several generations of the same family. Providing for the needs of a parent was simply considered a way of life.

The English Poor Laws of 1601 represented the first attempt to codify Western ideas of societal responsibilities for the welfare of all citizens. The 1601 laws brought together a number of Elizabethan Poor Laws that had been enacted since 1563 into one common law. These laws categorized the poor as deserving for the first time in history and required local taxation to provide care for those in need. It was these same concepts that were carried to the New World by the Pilgrims in 1620.

Throughout the 18th and 19th centuries, extended families continued to provide most of the care for aging family members. Those without family were provided for by community-based almshouses and poorhouses. This care usually amounted to warehousing at best and death sentences at their worst.   Relief was made as unpleasant and demeaning as possible in order to discourage dependency. It was not unusual to require a resident to wear a large "P" on their clothing in order to identify them to all as the resident of a poorhouse.

This method of caring for dependent elderly citizens worked, to some degree, as long as villages and towns remained small.   Colonial citizens felt obliged to help care for neighbors they had known their entire lives.   As villages grew to become towns, and towns became cities, individual commitment to caring for those in need diminished.   Citizens were less likely to have had a personal relationship with someone who may have come from the other side of town or only recently relocated to the community.

Following the Civil War, the speed of demographic change intensified.   During the 1870s and 1880s, important demographic changes occurred that would have a significant impact on how our society cared for the elderly in need. The Industrial Revolution, which followed the end of the Civil War, was marked by the greatest industrial expansion in the history of the world. Railroad lines connecting major cities made it possible to have factories of previously unimaginable size producing goods that would be shipped to cities a thousand miles away. These factories both attracted workers and displaced the traditional merchant craftsman. Local farms became less economical as Midwestern farmers were able to produce larger quantities in rich open fields and ship them to the cities.

For the first time, prosperity was not based solely on the efforts of the individual, but on economic conditions and management decisions that were outside the control of the wage earner. With decreased economic independence came a decreased ability to care for oneself, one's family, or others.

Young men flocked to the cities in search of stable industrial work and riches unimaginable on the farm. Many hoped to send for their families or return with enough money to care for them, but few ever did. The extended family, which had served young and old alike so well for generations, was now in decline. No longer could a parent or grandparent depend on living out their days in the home that they were born in, while their children and grandchildren ran the farm and provided them with care and support in their twilight years.

When coupled with the ongoing increases in average life expectancy, this meant that more and more elderly Americans were being left to fend for themselves as their children and grandchildren left for the cities. Those children who did remain behind endured the increased emotional and financial burden of caring for their parents or grandparents with fewer siblings nearby to assist.

This trend in urbanization continued throughout the 20th century. Even in 1890, near the end of the industrial revolution, only twenty eight percent of the population lived in cities. 1920 became a turning point in our nation's history when, for the first time, more than one half of all Americans resided in cities. By the start of the Great Depression, fifty six percent of the population had abandoned rural life and moved to cities throughout the United States. These cities were ill prepared, and lacked the necessary resources, to deal with the needs of the aging. Those left back on the farm were often no better prepared because of the sudden demographic changes to their extended families.

The financial upheaval of the Great Depression and the Dust Bowl left many unable to care for themselves, let alone others. Many who had moved to the cities could no longer find employment, banks foreclosed on farms, and the overuse and mismanagement of the western farm lands led to a dislocation of farming families as never before seen. For the first time in history, a large percentage of the American population was unable to provide for the basic needs of their families.

The outbreak of all-out war in Europe was the only thing that was finally able to restart the factories of the United States and return reasonable levels of employment and financial independence to many Americans.

Following the war, American factories turned to producing consumer goods. With the near total destruction of industrial capabilities throughout Europe and Asia, American factories were able to produce goods at record levels. The demand for labor to keep these factories running led to increased wages and stability for workers. Former servicemen began taking advantage of the GI bill to attend colleges that they could not have afforded before the war, and going on to secure well paying jobs upon graduation.

For the first time in our nation's history, millions of Americans were earning more than subsistence level pay. Homes were purchased, cars were financed, and families once again had the resources to care for their parents and grandparents. For some, this was a return to the agrarian ideal of living in a multigenerational home with each member of the family helping however they could.

As time went on, however, many middle class families found that they had the financial resources to care for their extended families, but neither the time nor ability to provide the care themselves. The increase in mobility, double income families, and divorce rates, meant that fewer and fewer disabled elderly had a family environment available where someone would be home all day to provide for their care.

As a result, the 1960's and 1970's saw an increase in the number of skilled nursing facilities or "Nursing Homes" throughout the United States. Much of this was due to Medicaid legislation passed in 1965, which provided federal grants to states that would fund medical assistance to elderly constituents of limited financial means. For those who had some degree of financial security, however, the legislation required a significant spending down of assets prior to becoming eligible for government funding.

Society had come a long way from the almshouses and poorhouses of Colonial times. Under Medicaid protection, no elderly American in need was left to fend for them self simply because they lacked the means. The financial boom of the 1950s and 1960s created what would become the most affluent elderly society ever by the mid 1980s. These were the individuals who had weathered the Great Depression and fought in two World Wars. They had invested their assets wisely, and had lived a modest life. However, many faced the possibility of losing all of their hard-earned savings to cover nursing home costs.

Even worse, the required spending down of assets often denied the surviving spouse financial security and essential resources. The "comfortable" retirement that so many had planned, sacrificed, and saved for, could be forever altered by a stroke, fall or cardiac event.

Life insurers and financial planners saw a societal need that they believed could be satisfied by the creation of a unique insurance product. Insurers had already helped millions of Americans address the problems of excessive estate taxes through the use of life insurance for estate planning. Now was the time to find a way to help protect against the unknown cost of Long Term Care.

Early products did little to provide significant protection of assets, but were an important step in the right direction. These policies limited care to skilled nursing facilities. Additionally, that care needed to immediately follow a hospitalization of three or more days. Benefits were only provided for a limited period of six to twelve months. These policies satisfied the need for limited stays following an acute illness or event, but did little to protect the assets of those with chronic and slowly progressive, debilitating diseases and disorders. Furthermore, these policies did nothing for those who wished to remain in their own homes while receiving care.

By the late 1980s, the LTC products that we see today began to emerge. These new products were more comprehensive. Coverage was available to provide both skilled care in a facility as well as care in the home. These policies would enable more of our senior citizens to "age in place" rather than suffer the emotional turmoil of relocation to a nursing home.

The societal costs of Long Term Care are tremendous as well. Indications are that these will only grow worse as our baby boomers continue to age and begin utilizing more Long Term Care services. Even with Medicare and Medicaid providing a significant percentage of Long Term Care funding, it continues to represent the single largest out-of-pocket medical expense for the elderly, with nearly one half of all costs paid for by the patients and their families.

The indirect cost of Long Term Care is more difficult to measure. The time required by informal caregivers and family members is staggering. Lost wages and productivity of spouses and children who are caring for loved ones are high. Perhaps most important, time that should be spent enjoying the final years with a loved one is too often spent as their caregiver.

Currently, only about two percent of all Long Term Care costs are funded by private insurance plans. This percentage is expected to increase substantially as the five percent of seniors with policies age to the point where they will begin needing assistance, and more of the market understands and accepts the need for Long Term Care insurance. The remainder of costs for care is either out of pocket, or funded by Medicare or Medicaid.

Medicare and Medicaid

"The test of our progress is not whether we add more to the abundance of those who have much; it is whether we provide enough for those who have too little."

Franklin D. Roosevelt

Recognition of societal responsibility for the aged and frail evolved from the English Poor Laws of 1601, to the New Deal reforms of the Great Depression, and on to the Great Society programs of the Johnson administration. Medicare and Medicaid are perhaps the most groundbreaking of legislation. They are two very different programs that emerged as part of President Johnson's "Great Society." Although often thought of as sister programs, they are not twins. Each is unique in its design, intention and focus.

Medicare

Medicare is a social insurance program that was established under Title XVIII of the Social Security Act of 1965. Workers are required to contribute to the Medicare fund through payroll taxes during their earning years. In return, they are covered by Medicare (Part A), which provides basic hospital insurance when they turn 65. Supplementary medical insurance (Part B) is available upon retirement for an additional monthly premium.

Each state manages its own Medicare plan, which means that the amounts and types of coverage vary significantly from one state to another. Medicare generally offers short-term rehabilitative home and institutional care but does not include Long Term Care.

Home care services are normally limited to skilled nursing care and rehabilitation. Medicare pays for a limited period of time to assist those who are expected to improve by receiving such benefits. Once an individual has stabilized with little chance for continued improvement, Medicare generally discontinues home care coverage.

Additionally, a disability must be severe enough to render the individual homebound in order to qualify for home care services under Medicare. Medicare considers one to be homebound if leaving the home would require a substantial effort and generally occurs only to attend religious services or a medical appointment.

Medicare may cover acute stays in a nursing facility but will generally limit the care that is provided to skilled nursing care only. Care must follow a period of hospitalization of at least three days. Medicare will then pay for the first 20 days of care at 100 percent, but will require a high deductible for nursing home care between the 20th and 100th day. Medicare does not pay for any nursing home care beyond the 100th day, nor would it pay to provide purely custodial care.

Medicaid

Medicaid was established in Title XIX of the Social Security Act of 1965. This program was designed as a joint venture between the federal and state governments to provide medical assistance for individuals and families with low income and resources. Available medical assistance includes nursing home coverage, but rarely provides for assisted living facility or other community-based programs.

Under the joint federal and state program, the federal government provides substantial financial assistance to the states, as well as broad-based guidelines for administering Medicaid. Each individual state establishes its own eligibility standards, and determines what type of services will be paid for, as well as the amount, duration and scope of these services. This has led to significant disparity between states.

Unlike Medicare, which is an insurance program, Medicaid is a welfare program intended to assist those truly unable to provide for themselves. In order to ensure that the system is not abused by those who can afford to pay for their own care, each state has set income and asset requirements. Initially, families were required to spend down nearly all of their assets in order to receive Medicaid. The Medicare Catastrophic Act of 1988 later modified the degree to which recipients had to spend down their assets.

The Medicare Catastrophic Act of 1988, which included Medicaid provisions, provided new eligibility guidelines designed to prevent spousal impoverishment. These guidelines recognized that, although one spouse might require confinement in a nursing facility, the assets and income of the spouse remaining in the community needed greater protection than previously afforded.

Understanding that variations may occur from state to state, a typical program has been outlined as follows:

Responsibility: To the extent possible, an individual is expected to pay for his or her own care. The program pays for those who can't afford it, or for those who have spent down their income and assets to a predetermined level.

Income: An individual receiving Medicaid assistance is permitted to keep roughly $30 per month in income. The remainder must go towards their care. When the beneficiary is married, a portion of their income may be added to the spouse's (provided that they too are not confined) up to a total income of approximately $1,400 per month for the spouse.

Assets: Medicaid recipients are also required to spend down their accumulated assets before the state will take over the cost of their care. Generally, these assets must be reduced to no more than $2,000 in cash, plus one's home, tangible personal belongings and a vehicle. Individuals are also allowed to have limited burial funds set aside for their final expenses.

In the case of the married couple, the assets are divided equally, regardless of owner, and the spouse living at home is allowed to keep one-half of all assets up to a maximum of between $18,132 and $90,660 (for 2003) depending on the state.

Many families try to avoid paying their share of nursing home expenses by hiding or transferring assets prior to requiring care. In order to prevent these abuses, states can "look back" to find transfers of assets for 36 months prior to the date the individual is institutionalized or the date he or she applies for Medicaid, whichever is later. For certain situations, this "look back" may extend for up to 60 months.

Those individuals who have improperly transferred assets in order to have Medicaid begin funding their care earlier are subject to penalties. The penalty is normally having to pay for the equivalent number of months that those assets would have paid for at fair market value.

Federal law also requires that the states seek to recover Medicaid payments from the assets of a deceased Medicaid recipient. This means that assets such as the home, that are exempt from the asset test while the recipient is living, could be subject to a Medicaid lien upon his or her death.

Since programs and provisions vary considerably from state to state, individuals are encouraged to consult their estate planning attorney or financial advisor before making any decisions regarding Medicaid. It is important that consumers understand their states required spend-down limits and penalties before considering Medicaid as an alternative to private insurance.

Early Long Term Care Policies

*"If at first you don't succeed. Try, try again.
Then quit. No use being a damn fool about it."*

W.C. Fields

The government plan for protecting senior citizens in need of care was ground-breaking and honorable. It provided a baseline of care and helped limit the number of older Americans left to fend for themselves at a time when they could least afford it. In turn, the government retained the right to recover its costs from any assets remaining upon the death of the individual.

This effectively worked as a payout for the absolute poor, and as a cash advance for those of modest means with assets that, once liquidated, could have paid for much of their care. For many in the middle- and upper-income classes, the cost of care would fall entirely on them and their families.

Complicating this matter further was the tremendous variation among states in how Medicaid was managed. Also, there were and are concerns about the long-term solvency of the program. By the mid 1970's, it was clear that additional alternatives to the system were needed.

Elderly and soon-to-be-elderly consumers began to understand the limitations of the system. Americans developed doubts that the government would be able to continue current levels of funding and support as the wave of baby boomers aged and began to utilize already-strained resources. No one wanted to return to the days when their life savings were entirely consumed, and they were unable to live out their last days in dignity.

Insurers, who were already quite active and effective in the area of estate planning and asset protection, began to look for ways to solve the problem. They began developing a new product for those who wanted to better protect themselves and their estates. This was risky because the insurers had no actual experience to base their products and pricing on, and few statistics on which to base estimates.

What first emerged was a courageous step in the right direction, but it would hardly qualify as Long Term Care insurance as we know it today. In fact, the earliest private insurance policies only provided six to twelve months of protection. Coverage was only provided for confinement in a nursing home following a hospital stay of at least three days. In essence, these policies acted as a limited expansion of the Medicare program.

Coverage would be highly effective for those who suffered an acute or traumatic event such as a broken hip or heart attack. Most of these individuals would fulfill the three-day hospitalization requirement. Furthermore, many would be expected to fully, or at least partially, recover to the point where they could return home, with some assistance from family and friends prior to the benefit running out.

For those individuals with chronic or progressive impairments, such as Parkinson's Disease or dementia, the policies were of limited value. These consumers would not normally be hospitalized prior to needing assistance. Furthermore, once they did go into the nursing home, the stay could last many years. In such cases, the six-to-twelve month benefits did little to protect the assets of the insured over the long term.

Advances in medicine also limited utilization of these early policies. Arthroscopic surgical techniques greatly diminished the recovery time leading to fewer hospitalizations that would last three days. Surgeries that had once required a hospital stay of a week or more were now being done on an outpatient basis. Increased use of physical and occupational therapy, coupled with advances in assistive devices for the elderly, meant that fewer elderly would require confined care, but many more would need assistance in their homes.

Over time, insurers came to better understand the needs of the consumer as well as the risks associated with longer term benefits. Market pressures eventually led to comprehensive products that would provide nursing facility care, or assistance for those who chose to remain in their homes and age in place for as long as possible. The following chapter outlines the more common terms and provisions of today's Long Term Care policies.

Today's Long Term Care Policies

*"There are no secrets to success.
It is the result of preparation,
hard work, learning from failure."*

General Colin Powell

Policies have continued to evolve into the forms that we see today, and will no doubt evolve further. Future policy offerings will be based on a combination of consumer needs and historical industry experience.

Although the coverage available today continues to vary, a core set of product features has begun to emerge. This chapter examines the most common features available as well as the advantages and limitations of each.

Tax Qualified vs. Non Qualified Contracts

The wave of baby boomers heading into their retirement years has been a great concern to the government for quite some time. By the mid 1990s the federal government understood that the wave of baby boomers, which had strained educational budgets in the 1960s and 1970s, was capable of bankrupting the Medicare and Medicaid budgets in the first half of the 21st century. Increased utilization of private Long Term Care insurance was seen as one way to lessen the financial burden on government.

22

The Health Insurance Portability and Accountability Act (HIPAA) of 1996 included the first federal guidelines that dealt with the issue of Long Term Care. That legislation provided a codification of Long Term Care provisions as well as tax incentives to purchase federally qualified Long Term Care policies.

In order to receive the favorable tax status outlined in HIPAA, tax qualified or "TQ" plans had to include very specific benefit eligibility criteria which the government defines as follows:

1) *The insured must be expected to be unable to perform at least 2 of 5 or more (usually 2 of 6) activities of daily living.*
2) *The insured must be diagnosed with such severe cognitive impairment that it is determined they are a threat to themselves or others.*
3) *The insured must also have a 90-day certification of expected need for care.*

HIPAA regulations allow tax-qualified policyholders to deduct some or all of their premiums if the insured itemizes deductions and their total deductible medical expenses exceed more than 7.5% of adjusted gross income. Additionally, the government has stated that tax-qualified Long Term Care benefits (up to a stated level which increases annually) are not subject to federal income taxation.

Critics of the tax-qualified plans argue it is doubtful that the government would actually tax the benefits of non-qualified plans. This remains an item for debate and clarification. Some argue that the generally tighter benefit criteria associated with the tax qualified plans, in addition to only paying for care that is expected to last 90 days or more, reduces the number of insureds who would be eligible for benefits sufficiently enough to outweigh the potential tax advantages.

Non-qualified plans do not require a 90-day certification of expected need. This allows some individuals who purchase shorter elimination periods to receive benefits even when the need may only last a couple of weeks or months. Non-qualified plans may utilize a more "liberal" trigger, such as an inability to perform 1 of 5 activities of daily living. They may also allow for benefits that a physician determines to be medically necessary.

Both designs have advantages as well as limitations. To determine which plan best suits their individual needs, consumers should take the time to read through the literature provided by the insurance companies, read the actual policy forms, and discuss the various options with their agent or financial planner.

Reimbursement vs. Indemnity

Long Term Care benefits may be payable as either a reimbursement of actual charges or as a set cash (indemnity) payment.

The reimbursement model is the most common method of benefit payment available today. Under this type of benefit structure, the insurance company would reimburse the claimant for all eligible expenses incurred up to a predetermined amount. Benefits might be paid to the insured, but would most commonly be assigned directly to the care provider.

Under the reimbursement model, the benefit paid would never be greater than the contractual daily (weekly or monthly) benefit, but may be considerably less if the actual cost of care is lower.

> *For Example:* *Rosemary Duggan has a reimbursement policy covering up to $150 per day of home care expense. When she submits her claim for home care following a hip replacement, it is determined that she requires assistance two hours per day for bathing and dressing. The actual cost for each visit is only $50 per day. Under a reimbursement plan, the insurer would pay $50. The remainder would either be lost, or most likely be carried in the policy to be used at a later point.*

Should the claim be for an amount greater than the maximum daily benefit, the difference would need to be paid out of pocket by the insured.

> *For Example:* *Joanne Spears has a reimbursement policy for $150 per day, but is confined to an Alzheimer's unit of a nursing home at a cost of $200 per day. In this situation, the policy would pay $150 per day, and the insured would be responsible to the nursing home for the remaining $50 per day.*

It is important to note that there are variations to the preceding two scenarios. Some policies pay a weekly benefit that will allow carryover of an unused daily benefit within any seven-day period. This is especially useful for home care claims when the care provided may vary from day to day. Benefits would be averaged over the week and paid up to a total of the daily benefit multiplied by seven.

The indemnity, or cash payment, type of policy helps to limit the confusion and uncertainty of benefits described previously, but generally has a more expensive premium than the reimbursement model. Under the indemnity structure, a predetermined cash benefit would be paid regardless of the actual cost of care. Most require that some degree of actual care be provided, but some only require that the insured be unable to perform two or more Activities of Daily Living (ADL) or be cognitively impaired.

> *For Example*: *Consider the previous example of Rosemary Duggan. Under an indemnity plan, the insurer would pay the entire $150 per day, even though her cost of care is only $50.*

Perhaps the greatest advantage of the indemnity model is that insureds are free to use the proceeds of their policy to purchase whatever care they deem necessary. Funds may be used for informal, unlicensed and alternative care that may not be covered under the reimbursement models. A cash benefit ensures that the policy keeps pace with changes in Long Term Care services. Early policies, for instance, had no provisions for assisted living facilities.

Due to the increased potential for abuse and misuse, indemnity policies are normally more expensive and underwritten more conservatively. The previous example provided Ms. Duggan $100 per day above the actual cost of care. This increase in cash may serve as a "disincentive" for Ms. Duggan to quickly recover from her surgery. For this reason, indemnity type claims would be expected to last longer and cost more.

Benefit Eligibility Triggers

With any insurance policy, certain events must occur or conditions exist in order to "trigger" the payment of benefits. Unlike life insurance benefits, which are paid upon the death of the insured, Long Term Care payouts are triggered by far more subjective criteria.

Benefit triggers vary by company, but are more consistent since the government established clear triggers in order for a policy to meet the criteria for tax-qualified status.

Under tax-qualified policies, the insured must be unable to perform at least 2 of 5, but usually 2 of 6, Activities of Daily Living (ADLs) or be cognitively impaired. Activities of Daily Living are defined as:

Bathing: Washing oneself by sponge bath, or in either a tub or shower, including the task of getting into or out of the tub or shower.
Continence: The ability to maintain control of bowel and bladder functions, or when unable to maintain control of bowel or bladder function, the ability to perform associated personal hygiene (including caring for catheter or colostomy bag).

Dressing: Putting on and taking off all items of clothing and any necessary braces, fasteners or artificial limbs.

Eating: Feeding oneself by getting food into the body from a receptacle (such as a plate, cup or table) or by feeding tube or intravenously.

Toileting: Getting to and from the toilet, getting on and off the toilet, and performing associated personal hygiene.

Transferring: Moving into or out of a bed, chair or wheelchair.

The cognitive trigger is usually defined as severe cognitive impairment requiring supervision to prevent injury to self or others.

Non-tax-qualified policies are not limited to the triggers outlined by the federal government. Many utilize the same triggers as the tax qualified policies, but a number of companies have developed their own triggers or continue to utilize triggers that predate tax-qualified legislation.

Some of the more common non-qualified benefit triggers are outlined below.

Limited ADL Triggers are used in some non-qualified plans. Whereas the industry standard is 2 of 6 ADLs, some insurers have chosen to offer benefits when the insured is unable to perform only 1 of 5 ADLs. Still others have defined the benefit trigger at 2 of 5 ADLs.

These differences are not as simple as they may first appear. Under most policies, the insured must be unable to perform 2 of 6 ADLs. Another way to look at this is an inability to perform 33% of the ADLs. The 1 of 5 ADL trigger (20%) may seem easier to satisfy, but most times bathing is the ADL dropped from the list, as it is usually the first ADL lost.

The 2 of 5 (40%) ADL trigger, on the other hand, is more difficult to satisfy. These also routinely remove bathing from the list, which, in effect, makes the trigger a 3 of 6 (50%) for many individuals.

Medical Necessity triggers continue to be available on a number of older Long Term Care policies as well as on a handful of current products. Under most medical necessity triggers, the insured is eligible for benefits if their personal physician determines that the care is "medically necessary." There are wide variations in the language of this trigger. Some versions substantially limit the degree of control that the insurer has in managing the claim.

Because of the potential for abuse, some of the more recent policies utilizing the medical necessity trigger limit its use to the nursing home portion of the contract.

Another type of non tax-qualified trigger is based upon a list of Instrumental Activities of Daily Living or IADLs.

IADL triggers are far less common and appear to be quickly vanishing from the Long Term Care insurance market. Under the terms of this trigger, benefits would be paid if it is determined the insured is unable to perform a number of instrumental activities of daily living.

The use of IADLs as a benefit trigger is often coupled with an ADL trigger and/or limited to pre-specified services or features of the policy. The IADLs are defined as follows:

Transport: The ability to drive or make own arrangements to use public transportation. Getting to or from as well as in and out of a vehicle without assistance.

Shopping: Getting to and from shops and buying goods. Returning home and storing goods without assistance.

Housework: Keeping the house cleaned with dusting, vacuuming, and maintaining hygiene in the kitchen and bathroom without assistance.

Meal Preparation: Preparing a complete meal independently.

Laundry: Regularly laundering clothes and bedding without assistance.

Finances: Handling personal banking and bill payments without assistance.

Taking Medication: Managing to maintain a prescribed drug regimen without assistance or prompting.

Using the Telephone: Able to use the telephone appropriately without assistance.

Self-Admission trigger. In recent years a few companies have experimented with a self-admission trigger for nursing home portions of the policy. Under this plan, the insured has full authority to determine if they need to be admitted to a nursing home. The theory behind the use of this trigger is that very few individuals would admit themselves to a nursing home without truly needing the care.

Types of Benefits

Today's policies have a number of features available to the consumer. Each company tries to differentiate itself from others by including unique features or options. However, the basic benefits available are reasonably consistent from company to company.

Most products available today are structured around a confined care, or facility, provision that provides coverage for both nursing homes and assisted living facilities. This product can sometimes be purchased alone, or as the base portion of a comprehensive Long Term Care policy.

Community-based services are usually combined with the confined care provision to form what is referred to as a comprehensive Long Term Care policy. A few insurers offer community-based coverage on a stand-alone basis without the underlying facility benefits. This is becoming less common due to generally "poor" industry experience.

Community-based benefits are designed and intended to help policyholders age in place while theoretically decreasing the cost of care for the insurer. There are a number of features included in the standard community-based provision. The most common features are outlined below.

Home Health Care: *Provides for skilled nursing and home health aide care to assist the individual with their activities of daily living.*

31

Homemaker Benefit: Provides for assistance with instrumental activities of daily living. Most policies require that the individual is receiving skilled care in order to exercise this benefit.

Adult Day Care: Provides benefits for care in an adult day care facility. This benefit is especially useful for seniors living with their working adult children.

Hospice Benefit: Provides coverage for admission into a hospice facility if the insured is determined to be terminally ill.

Alternate Plan of Care: This feature allows the insured and insurer to work together to provide services outside of those specifically stated in the policy. Services may be considered if financially advantageous to both the policyholder and insurer. An example of this might be the construction of a wheelchair ramp or home modifications that enable the individual to remain at home rather than being confined to a facility.

Most policies offer a number of other benefits in addition to the core of facility care and home health care components. Some of these benefits are built into the base policy, while others are available as optional benefits. The following is a list of some of the more common benefits available. When comparing policies, it is important to understand which benefits are built into the base policy and which are only available for an extra premium.

Waiver of Premium: Most policies have a waiver of premium provision. The standard waiver of premium provision will waive all premiums while *an insured is on claim and receiving benefits. This waiver may begin at the onset of claim or after a predetermined period such as 90 days.*

Waiver of Premium upon Death of Spouse: A number of policies available contain a benefit that will waive all future premiums upon the death of the insured's spouse. This generally requires that the spouse also be insured under the same or a similar contract with the same company.

Waiver of Premium if Spouse is on Claim: This benefit waives all premiums due while an insured's spouse is on claim and receiving benefits. This generally requires that the spouse also be insured under the same or a similar contract with the same company.

Inflation Protection (Simple): Provides for annual increases of a fixed percentage, usually five percent, of the base amount issued. Under this provision, a $100 per day benefit would be at $125 per day after 5 years. Premium rates will not increase for these increases as the premium for this is normally factored into the original policy rates.

Inflation Protection (Compound): Provides for annual increases of a fixed percentage, usually five percent, of the daily benefit in force at the time of increase. Under this provision a $100 per day benefit would be at $127.68 per day after 5 years. The further this is carried out, the greater the difference between simple and compound inflation. Premium rates will not *increase for these increases as the premium for this is normally factored into the original policy rates.*

Guaranteed Purchase Option: This benefit provides an alternative method of addressing inflation issues. Under the terms of the guaranteed purchase option, the insured is given an opportunity to increase their coverage every three years. The amount of increase is usually limited to fifteen percent per option, and additional premiums will only be charged if the insured chooses to accept the increase. Unlike the inflation protection options, these options are not normally available while on claim.

Caregiver Training Benefit: This benefit provides for training of a family member or informal caregiver. The cost of this training is normally limited to five times the daily benefit amount. It is important to note that whereas many insurers will pay for the cost of caregiver training, most would not pay the informal caregiver for services provided after training is complete.

Respite Care: Most policies include a respite benefit in order to relieve the informal caregiver or family member from the stress of care. Under the respite provision, the policy would pay for someone to come into the home for a limited period, usually 21 days per calendar year, in order to provide relief for the informal caregiver.

Bed Reservation Benefit: This provision enables the insured to keep his or her bed in a nursing facility in the event that they require hospitalization. This benefit is normally limited to a period of 21 days per calendar year.

Durable Medical Equipment Benefit: Some policies allow a limited multiple of the daily benefit to be used for renting or purchasing durable medical equipment that is needed to assist the insured with activities of daily living. This may include such items as a walker, wheelchair, or other assistive device.

Return of Premium: A number of companies offer a return of premium rider for an additional cost. These riders vary from company to company, but generally allow a refund of part or all of the paid premium every set number of years, usually ten, provided that no claims have been paid.

Return of Premium upon Death: Similar to the return of premium rider, this benefit refunds some or all of the premiums paid. Instead of refunding the premium every ten years; however, the premium is refunded to the insured's beneficiary or estate upon their death. Most insurers require that the policy have been in force for a number of years, normally between five and ten, before this provision would pay.

Nonforfeiture: Tax Qualified legislation requires insurers to offer a nonforfeiture provision intended to provide some protection to the insured in the event of the policy lapsing. The terms of this rider usually require the policy to be in force for at least three years. Should the policy lapse after that point, the insured would be entitled to benefits up to the lesser of the sum of all premiums paid or 30 times the daily benefit.

Contingent Nonforfeiture Benefit: Many insurers offer an alternative form of nonforfeiture benefit. These riders expand on the traditional nonforfeiture by allowing an additional option of reducing the policy benefits in the event that premium rates increase above a predetermined level. For instance, an individual with a $200-per-day benefit may get the choice of a 20% rate increase or 20% reduction in benefits for the same rate.

Optional or supplemental benefits continue to evolve. Furthermore, insurers continue to redefine and clarify these benefits as experience accumulates. Therefore, the preceding list should not be considered all inclusive. The consumer is advised to discuss all available options with his or her agent or financial planner in order to determine which best suit their needs.

Each consumer should take the time to carefully read the policy language associated with any policy provision or optional benefit and question his or her financial planner or insurance agent as to the meaning and relative value of each before making a final decision.

Daily Benefit Amount

Determining the amount of benefits to purchase is very important and extremely difficult. Purchasing too little coverage may significantly diminish the value of obtaining Long Term Care insurance. In such a situation, the insured would still be required to spend down his or her assets to address the difference between the actual cost of care and the insured coverage before being eligible for Medicaid.

As with many other types of insurance, purchasing too high of a benefit only serves to unnecessarily increase premiums without actually increasing protection. This concern is far more significant for a reimbursement policy than for an indemnity policy and is somewhat negated by policies that utilize a "pool of money" approach which preserves any unused dollars for future use.

Although benefits may be stated in terms of daily, weekly, or monthly amounts, most policies available today express benefits in terms of daily benefit amounts. Additionally, some companies allow the insured to choose different amounts for nursing home care than for home care. Under most options, the home care portion is less than or equal to the nursing home portion as the cost of home care is generally less.

The maximum daily benefit available may be as high as $500 per day depending upon the insurance company. Few insurers, however, issue above $300 per day.

Determining what maximum daily benefit to purchase is largely an issue of geography. Buyers in the Northeast, for instance, would generally need to purchase a higher maximum daily benefit than those in the Midwest. Most consumers can get a reasonable approximation of what benefit amount should be purchased by following four simple steps:

Step 1: *Determine the current cost of care* in the purchaser's area. The consumer should do some research regarding actual cost of nursing homes, assisted living facilities and skilled home care providers near his or her place of residence. Some of this information may be found on the Internet or gathered with a few simple phone calls.

Step 2: *Estimate the effect of inflation* on the current cost of care. Health care costs continue to rise at rates greater than that of inflation in general, and this trend is expected to continue for some time into the future. For most purchasers, there will be many years between the time of purchase and a possible claim. Inflation over these years will tend to devalue the benefits of the policy, unless the policy contains an inflation protection provision. The impact of inflation would be far greater for younger purchasers than for those already in their 80s.

Step 3: *Evaluate the possibility of relocation* to another geographic region of the country. Our society is increasingly mobile and many individuals may not claim from the same location where they purchased their policy.

Consumers should make an honest attempt to anticipate the potential for a move. Retiring from a location such as southwestern Connecticut to southern Florida may have a significant impact on the cost of care. Also, it is not uncommon to relocate closer to children once the need for care is identified. All policies will pay benefits regardless of the state of residence at the time of claim.

Step 4: Determine affordability of the product. Long Term Care policies are expensive. A number of companies have required rate increases over time. Purchasing a top-of-the-line policy is of little value if the policy lapses before benefits are needed. A number of states require insurers to provide the prospective customer with a Long Term Care suitability form. This form is intended to help the consumer determine if the cost of the product is reasonable, given his or her assets and income.

Few buyers have an unlimited source of income. The consumer is best advised to conduct his or her own research and then balance actual needs with the available products.

Elimination Periods

Elimination, or waiting, periods are an important aspect of an LTC policy. Consumers can think of elimination periods as "deductible" periods during which they must pay the expenses incurred. As with medical, dental, auto, homeowners and other forms of insurance which utilize deductibles, the price of insurance decreases as the deductible amount increases.

Unlike most other forms of insurance, the deductible amount is normally measured in days rather than dollars. The most common elimination or deductible periods for Long Term Care insurance are 0 days, 20 or 30 days, 60 days, and 90 or 100 days.

Not all elimination periods are created equally. The consumer needs to carefully read the policy in order to understand exactly what is meant by the elimination period. Elimination periods can either be measured by service days or calendar days. Each has different claim experience, and therefore different costs associated.

<u>For Example:</u> Suppose Florence Cullen and Margaret Sullivan each have a Long Term Care policy with a 60 day elimination period, and each woman falls and breaks her hip. If Florence's policy contains a service day provision, she will need to receive home care for 60 service days before the insurer will begin making payments. Since Florence has friends and family that can assist her, she only needs a licensed home health aide three mornings a week to assist her with bathing and dressing. At this rate, it will take 20 weeks (140 days) for Florence to satisfy her elimination period and for the insurer to begin paying benefits.

Margaret, on the other hand, purchased a policy that counts calendar days toward her elimination period. She too only needs a bathing and dressing visit three mornings a *week. In her case, however, the insurer begins paying for her care on the 61st day, after only 25 home health aide visits.*

Elimination periods are further complicated by the type utilized by the insurer. It is not uncommon, for example, for insurance policies to have a "lifetime" elimination period. In such cases, the elimination period need only be satisfied once during the life of the policy. This means that subsequent periods of ADL dependence would not require an out-of-pocket payment prior to the insurer paying for care.

This is not, however, a universal feature, and the buyer should be careful to understand how the provision works. Alternative policy provisions require that the insured pay for care through the elimination period for each period of care. Some providers choose a hybrid approach, which allows for a lifetime elimination period for nursing home or facility care, but requires that the elimination period be re-satisfied for each new home care claim.

Although the practice is diminishing, many insurers have also developed provisions that waive, or substantially reduce, the elimination period as encouragement for the insured to utilize their care management services in the event of a claim. The theory behind this is that by getting involved in the claim early, the insurer is able to secure discount service providers and help assist the claimant back to recovery.

The requirements for tax-qualified status also complicate the issue of elimination periods. Tax-qualified policies require a certification that care is expected to be needed for at least 90 days in order to receive benefits. This means that, even with a 0 or 20 day elimination period, benefits would not be paid for care that is only expected to be needed for 60 or 70 days. This should be understood by anyone purchasing a tax-qualified policy with a benefit period of less than 90 days.

For Example: *Suppose that two sisters, Mary and Louise Duffy (ages 77 and 79, respectively) each purchase Long Term Care policies for $100 per day with a zero day elimination period and a two-year benefit period. Mary chooses to purchase a tax-qualified plan, while Louise decides to purchase a non tax-qualified plan.*

Regrettably, Mary and Louise are both out for a walk when Louise slips on ice, taking Mary down with her. Both women suffer fractured ankles and need assistance bathing and dressing each morning. Upon investigation of the claims, both require care, but neither is expected to require it for more than 90 days.

Under the 90-day certification provision of the tax qualified policy, Mary's care will not be reimbursed. Louise, on the other hand, has no such provision and therefore would be reimbursed for her expenses. Should Mary's care exceed 90 days, however, the insurer would then reimburse her expenses back to the first day of claim.

It is important that consumers understand elimination periods and think of them more as deductible periods. The buyer must understand that benefits will not be paid for any care received prior to the satisfaction of the elimination period. One common misconception is that once the elimination period has been satisfied, benefits will be paid retroactively to the inception of the claim. This will not happen.

Benefit Periods

The next factor that should be taken into consideration is how long of a benefit period to purchase. The benefit period is the length of time that a claim will be paid. Depending on the insurer, this can be expressed as either a time frame (days or years), or in dollars. The latter is referred to as the "pool of money" approach. Like all aspects of a Long Term Care policy, this decision comes down to a cost/benefit calculation.

A service day benefit period would count each day, or portion thereof, towards the maximum benefit period. In this case, the entire day would count as a benefit day if any care is provided, regardless of the amount of care received.

For Example: Charles Grande purchased a Long Term Care policy for $100 per day, with a 20-day elimination period and two-year benefit period, which was based upon service days. Following his stroke, Charles required assistance from a home health aide for four hours per day, seven days a week. This care is expected to last indefinitely. The cost of this care was $18 per hour.

43

Even though Charles purchased a policy with a two-year benefit period for $100 per day, for a total of $73,000, his benefits were terminated after only receiving $52,560 at the end of his two-year benefit.

Most policies' benefits today are expressed in terms of a pool of money. Under the "pool of money" approach, the benefit is expressed as a dollar amount equal to the maximum daily benefit, multiplied by the number of benefit days purchased.

To continue the previous example: Had Charles purchased the contract with a pool of money benefit, he would still have $20,440 remaining to help pay for his Long Term Care expenses. At his current expenditure of $36 per day, this buys him an additional 568 days of claim reimbursement or essentially extends his benefit from two years to three and a half years.

The cost of coverage increases, though not proportionately, as the benefit period increases. The most common benefit periods available today are two years, three years, five years and Lifetime or Unlimited. A number of companies also offer four- and six-year benefit options.

In addition to understanding how the policy benefit period would be administered, consumers should familiarize themselves with any *restoration of benefit* provision available. Although terms may vary, the restoration provision enables the policy to "reset" itself to initial value should the insured recover and maintain a period, usually 180 days, of ADL independence.

Premium Rates

*"The cynic knows the price of everything
and the value of nothing."*

Oscar Wilde "Lady Windemere's Fan"

The consumer would not be expected to understand all of the pricing considerations of a Long Term Care product. They would benefit, however, from a baseline understanding of how a policy is priced and what that may mean for them.

Most important, the consumer needs to understand that Long Term Care policies are "guaranteed renewable". This means that, although the insurer can never cancel or alter the policy, other than for non-payment of premium or exhausting the policy benefits, premium rates are subject to change and can be increased over time.

Insurers, however, are not free to increase rates indiscriminately. An increase in rates must be for everyone insured within a given policy or policy class. Additionally, increases must be submitted to, and approved by, each state's Department of Insurance. Obtaining these increases is not easy, and individual states may decide to deny or reduce the requested increase, if they are not convinced that it is necessary or that the increase is for an unacceptable reason.

Some consumer groups believe that it is best to stay away from insurers that have required premium rate increases on past policies. While this may be an important factor, it is no guarantee of future actions. The lack of a rate increase may be indicative of an insurer's stability and understanding of the product, or may instead represent a failure of the insurer to recognize and address problems as they materialize.

The guaranteed renewable aspect of Long Term Care insurance serves an important purpose. Without it, no insurer could take the risk of offering the coverage at all. Long Term Care is a relatively new insurance product. Furthermore, it is an insurance product that has constantly changed throughout its short existence. This leaves the actuaries with very little credible evidence as to the appropriateness of their pricing assumptions. The ability to change rates as experience materializes enables the insurance companies to offer the product to millions of consumers who desire it, without risking financial insolvency.

Pricing

When developing premium rates, the actuary must consider a number of important items that consumers rarely consider. They must bear in mind that, unlike many other forms of insurance that are annually renewable, LTC policies represent a long-term commitment to the insured. Unlike automobile insurance and homeowners insurance, which can be terminated by the insurer at the end of any given policy year, Long Term Care insurance can only be terminated by the insurer for non-payment of premiums. Therefore, any mistake that the actuary may make in pricing is one that could have lasting repercussions.

The actuary also understands that, sooner or later, many of those insured will file a claim if they live long enough. The actuaries depend on the underwriter to limit the number of early claims by screening out those who are predisposed to developing debilitating illnesses or may already be in need of assistance. Of those that are insurable, the actuary must factor in assumptions about how many will die without ever requiring benefits and how many are likely to let their policies lapse. A miscalculation in either of these factors could mean that more people go on to claim than anticipated, and that premium rates would not be sufficient to cover all the claims.

Ideally, there will be many years between the time that a consumer buys an insurance policy and when a claim will emerge. The actuary assumes that these premiums are invested during that period of time and factors in that investment income into the ability to pay future claims. Determining the appropriate investment rate has a significant impact on both the price of the policy, as well as the ability to fund future claims. A one-percent change in the insurer's investment portfolio may have as much as a ten-percent impact on pricing due to long-term compounding.

Generally speaking, the actuary tries to price the policy so that the insurer will have a 60 percent loss ratio. This means that for every dollar received in premium, the insurer expects to pay out 60 cents in claims. The remaining 40 cents are needed to cover items such as product development, commissions, underwriting costs, policyholder services, claim administration fees, general overhead and profit margins.

Affordability

Many insurance companies and states have recognized the importance of determining the affordability of purchasing an LTC policy. Affordability is important to all lines of insurance, but especially important in LTC, where many policyholders are living on a fixed income while having to pay increased cost for health care and other services. It serves neither the insured nor the insurer to issue a policy to someone who cannot afford to keep the coverage in force for long.

This problem is compounded by the fact that rates for Long Term Care policies are not guaranteed. Although policies are priced with the intention of maintaining a level premium over the life of the policy, rate increases are not unheard of and may be quite steep at times.

Many states and insurance companies have developed suitability guidelines to help the consumer determine if he or she can truly afford the coverage. Unfortunately, there is little uniformity to these guidelines, which may be based on either income or net worth. As a rule of thumb, however, annual premiums in excess of seven percent of income or three percent of net worth would be of concern.

For Example: Steven and Grace Fargo are a 65-year-old couple applying for a $140 per day comprehensive LTC policy with a 60-day *elimination period and a five-year benefit period. The cost of their policies is $2,000 per year for each.*

The Fargo's are living on a retirement income of $32,000 per year. They also have nearly $185,000 in assets that they would like to preserve for each other and their children.

The $4,000 per year combined premium would consume more than twelve percent of their income. Additionally, the Fargo's need to consider how affordable the premium would be should the insurer require a rate increase of twenty percent or so. In such a case, the new premium of $4,800 per year would require fifteen percent of their earnings. This scenario may well lead to an eventual lapse and a poor investment for the Fargos.

Such a situation does not necessarily mean that this couple are not ideal candidates for Long Term Care insurance. Instead, they should consider alternatives that may lower their cost but still provide reasonable protection, such as a longer elimination period, shorter benefit period, lower daily benefit, or another insurance company.

An excessive premium to income or net worth ratio raises a number of serious issues. States are concerned that their LTC purchasing constituents (usually senior citizens) might be taken advantage of by being sold a policy they cannot afford that will lapse before they need it. Insurers are concerned that early lapses will cost them money due to the high cost of acquiring and issuing the policy that will not be recouped. The underwriters are concerned that a consumer willing to part with a high percentage of income may be doing so because of a known medical or cognitive impairment that places them at significant risk of claim.

Payment Options

Long Term Care insurance is expensive when compared to many other insurance products. The high cost of this coverage is of special significance when dealing with senior citizens living on a fixed, or often diminishing, income. To address this concern, a number of companies have developed a variety of payment options. The more common payment methods are outlined below.

Lifetime: Most policies issued today are sold with a level lifetime premium. This means that, assuming no rate increases are required, the consumer will pay a set premium for the remainder of his or her life. The actuaries have levelized the premium by charging more than is required for the actual risk during the insured's younger years in order to pre-fund the higher risk associated with aging in later years.

10 Pay: This limited pay option is especially attractive for younger consumers during their working years. This option requires a substantially higher premium for a shorter period of time. The benefit is that the insured will no longer need to pay premiums when living on a fixed or reduced retirement income.

<u>Paid up at 65:</u> Similar in concept to the 10 pay option, this payment method is designed to pre-fund the entire policy during the insured's working years.

<u>Single Pay:</u> Although very rare because of the tremendous initial premium involved, this payment option relies on a single initial payment to pre-fund the entire life of the policy. This may be attractive for executive compensation packages, or for a recently widowed individual who wishes to use a portion of the proceeds from the spouse's life insurance policy to ensure that they will have access to appropriate care as they continue to age.

It is important to note that there is no single best method for all consumers. These multiple payment options were developed to best serve the varied needs of all consumers. When considering which Long Term Care policy to purchase, individuals must determine for themselves which policy payment method makes the most sense for their financial situation.

__Underwriting__

"Take calculated risks. That is quite different from being rash"

General George S. Patton

In order to understand the underwriting process, one must first be familiar with the basic premise of insurance.

Insurance is a product designed to protect an individual, group, or business from an *unforeseen* risk by spreading the risk of loss over a number of lives. The word *unforeseen* is the key to this process, otherwise it would not be insurance.

Insurers know, with some degree of certainty, the likelihood that a specific incident will occur. As a result, the insurer is able to spread that risk among a number of individuals to minimize its impact.

For example: Suppose an insurer assumes that one out of every 10,000 healthy 42-year-old males will die this year. No one knows which of the 10,000 it will be. The financial loss to the family of that one individual could be devastating. The insurance concept is applied when the group determines that no single individual could or should bear that loss. If each of the 10,000 paid $10 into a pool at the start of the year, the pool would have $100,000 to provide for the family of the deceased.

52

This concept works well for all involved, and is considered equitable, assuming that all have approximately the same level of health. The system breaks down, however, when one member of the pool is aware of significant medical history that places him or her at a much higher risk of death than the others. This is where the role of underwriting comes in.

The underwriting process is necessary to analyze and segment individuals into appropriate risk classifications. It is also the most effective way to limit the number of people who would withhold important information in order to obtain insurance for which they may not otherwise qualify. The underwriter makes this determination by gathering medical and cognitive as well as non-medical information.

The Application

The application for insurance is normally the first source of information that the underwriter sees in evaluating each proposed insured for coverage. It is also the most important document since it is the basis for the insurance contract between the insurer and insured. The application is routinely made a part of the contract and will serve as the source document for any dispute that may arise in the future.

Applications vary considerably from company to company. Some insurers prefer a shorter application with fewer questions. These questions, however, are normally broader in scope. Others have developed lengthy questionnaires with detailed and specific questions.

Accurate and complete answers to all application questions will help to expedite the process. Contrary to popular belief, omitting information from an application does not always work to the advantage of the insured, but often to their disadvantage. Omitted history can substantially or indefinitely delay the underwriting process and raise questions of candor.

For example: Ellen O'Brien is filling out an application for Long Term Care insurance. One of the questions asked if, within the proceeding 12 months, the proposed insured had consulted or been treated by a physician. Suppose Ms. O'Brien had consulted her physician six weeks prior. If she writes "Dr. Smith six weeks ago," this may prompt the underwriter to order medical records from Dr. Smith, which would further delay the underwriting process. On the other hand, should Ms. O'Brien respond "consulted Dr. Smith six weeks ago for annual checkup: all results normal," the underwriter may be more inclined to accept the statement at face value and issue the policy.

Above all, it is important to recognize that all statements on the application become the basis for, and a part of, the legal contract between the insurer and insured. The last thing that either party wants to find out at claim time is that an individual did not disclose pertinent history on the application or provided false information, and the claim may not be paid as a result of that omission or misrepresentation.

Underwriting Requirements

In order to fully evaluate the proposed insured, the underwriter may order any number of requirements in order to develop, confirm, or clarify medical history, cognitive status and other non-medical issues. These requirements may be ordered based on set parameters, such as age or benefit applied for, or for specific reasons.

There are a number of potential requirements that an underwriter may choose to order on any given applicant for Long Term Care insurance. Some of the more common requirements are outlined below:

Telephonic Interview: Most LTC insurers use some form of telephone interview when evaluating many of their proposed insureds. These interviews routinely ask questions about medical history as well as non-medical issues such as activity level, living arrangements, marital status, and proximity to the proposed insured's children. A common interview will last between 15 and 30 minutes and may include a screening for cognitive status.

Face-to-Face Assessment: Many insurers also conduct face-to-face assessments on a subpopulation of applicants. This is based on age or is conducted to better understand a medical issue that was previously disclosed. Face-to-face assessments are usually conducted by a registered nurse in the home of the proposed insured. These assessments are designed to observe living conditions and the ability to function in all activities of daily living.

Cognitive Screen: By most reports, cognitive claims are the longest and most expensive for insurers. Because of this, it is especially important that underwriters make every effort to determine those who may be purchasing the policy due to the recognition of early cognitive impairments. As a result, the industry has borrowed or developed a number of screening tools that help to identify those at increased risk of cognitive impairment. These cognitive screens can be conducted either in person or over the phone.

Attending Physician's Statement: Medical records are an essential part of the underwriting process. Many insurers will obtain copies of a physician's records in order to better understand the health risk of the proposed insured. Records may be obtained based on age, medical history or the type of benefit applied for. They are commonly ordered for medical conditions, such as diabetes or cancer, for which the proposed insured may not be able to provide appropriate risk assessment information.

Lab Studies: Although rare, collecting blood and urine samples is becoming more common. These may be ordered to better assess diseases such as diabetes or alcoholism, or may be based on criteria such as age or benefit amount.

Motor Vehicle Report: Driving history may be a strong indicator of ADL and/or cognitive independence. These records are fast, easy *and inexpensive for the insurer to obtain. Some insurers obtain them at older ages in order to better assess cognition and physical ability. An individual who has had their license revoked or has been cited for numerous violations may represent increased risk to the insurer.*

Pharmacology Report: Pharmacological records are one of the most objective and potentially valuable underwriting requirements available today. The technology for this sort of search has recently become available and is still in a testing phase for many insurers.

Understanding the proposed insured's history of pharmaceutical use better enables the underwriter to assess the risk that he or she represents. A pharmacology report enables the underwriter to evaluate the proposed insured's medical history more objectively. It also provides important insight into an individual's compliance with their prescription medications.

Medical Information Bureau (MIB): MIB codes have long been used for underwriting life and disability insurance and are just now gaining acceptance among Long Term Care insurers. The MIB codes identify medical or other risk management concerns that another insurance company has already identified on a specific individual. These codes were designed to prevent individuals from applying to one company, and when declined, applying to another without fully sharing their history. The Medical Information Bureau has very strict rules for confidentiality and use of these codes and it regularly audits its member companies to ensure compliance.

Few applications would require all of the above underwriting measures. Each company determines the investigative tools that are the most appropriate and cost effective for the various categories of risk. Some companies may obtain physician reports on all applicants, while others on very few. Regardless of the type and number of requirements obtained, it is important to understand that the insurer is not attempting to pry into the private life of an applicant, but is simply making a serious attempt to obtain the same information that the proposed insured has when applying for insurance.

Types of Decisions

Long Term Care underwriting varies considerably from one company to another. Each company has determined its own tolerance for risk. This tolerance may be based on corporate philosophy, financial strength, experience in Long Term Care, or availability of reinsurance. Product features and premiums are also important factors in determining the risks that are acceptable.

The Long Term Care underwriter is more fortunate than those who underwrite most other products. The nature of the coverage allows for the utilization of more "tools" to custom tailor an offer to fit the needs of the proposed insured while protecting the company from excessive risk. The decision as to which tools to implement is part of the risk management philosophy of each company.

One of the most common misconceptions about Long Term Care insurance is that many people believe that they would be uninsurable in view of medical history such as a past heart attack or diabetes. This is rarely the case however, as many insurers have learned to better segment risk factors and are now able to offer coverage to a large number of people with chronic medical histories.

An outline of the more common underwriting decision tools follows. Each of these tools can be used separately or in conjunction with others.

Accept / Reject: A number of companies have chosen to take an "accept or reject" approach to offering coverage. In such cases, the proposed insured is either accepted as applied for or rejected.

Additional Ratings: Some medical conditions are of concern to underwriting specialists since the base product was not priced to cover individuals with a given history or condition such as obesity. Charging an additional premium for coverage enables the insurer to accept some, but not all, of the individuals who would otherwise be considered uninsurable under the pricing of the base policy.

Longer Elimination Periods: A proposed insured may also have a medical condition, such as moderate osteoarthritis, that represents a higher than acceptable risk of short-term claim, but an acceptable long-term risk. In such cases, the underwriter may determine that it is best to require a longer elimination period, such as 60 or 90 days, in order to decrease the likelihood of the arthritis triggering a short-term claim.

Shorter Benefit Periods: Other applicants, such as an individual at risk of stroke, may be insurable. However, if the condition leads to a claim, it would very likely be a long and expensive one. In such cases, the underwriter may limit the maximum exposure by offering a reduced benefit period such as two years.

Lower Daily Benefits: There may be factors in a case, such as a history of disability or questionable claim behavior, that might lead the underwriter to offer a reduced daily benefit. This may be done in order to limit liability or to limit the likelihood of abuse by necessitating a co-pay type of situation.

Limiting Features: Policyholders will always be more receptive to receiving home health service in their homes than being confined to a nursing facility. There are also a number of impairments, such as gait disturbances or visual disorders, that lend themselves to a high incidence of home care claims, but few nursing home claims. As a result, the underwriter may determine that it is best to limit the coverage to a confined care policy by removing the home and community care provisions.

Unfortunately, many agents and applicants for insurance view a counter-, or substandard, offer as negative. The truth is that the individual would still benefit from some form of coverage and, for many, the alternative to a counter-offer would be no insurance at all. Most insurers who have developed a counter-offer program have done so at great expense and risk so they can insure more individuals.

Claims Management

*"Health is not valued till
sickness comes."*

Thomas Fuller

Appropriate management of claims is an extremely critical aspect of the risk management process. The Claims Department is charged with one of the most difficult tasks in the life of the LTC policy. The responsibility of the claims operation is to pay all contractually appropriate claims, while investigating and screening out those that do not meet the claims criteria as stated in the policy.

Though this may sound harsh at first glance, the function is very reasonable. Companies who manage claims too loosely may suffer losses that can diminish their ability to stay in the business for the long term. This could negatively impact their policyholders in a variety of ways. The company may require a rate increase from all insureds to cover the cost of those claims that should have been denied, or the company may be unable to meet its future financial obligations to pay claims in years ahead.

Unlike a life, auto, or medical claim, Long Term Care claims are ongoing claims that are often quite complicated. Like most claims situations, the claims staff must first determine initial eligibility as previously outlined. However, unlike most other insurance products, the claims staff must continually re-evaluate the need and determine how much care an individual needs and how long they will need it for.

The skills required to investigate claims properly and the philosophy by which a company manages claims vary considerably across the industry. The type of investigation and degree of active claims management also differs according to the terms, specifically the claims triggers, within a given policy. There are, however, some practices that are common in the management of Long Term Care claims.

Determining Initial Eligibility

The Claims Department needs to review a number of factors to determine if an insured individual meets the benefit eligibility criteria. The first step is to identify the particular limitations and needs of the policyholder filing a claim.

The claim is normally initiated by a telephone call to the insurance company. This initial call may be from the insured, a family member, their insurance agent or even their physician. During this intake call, the claims staff gathers basic information to determine if the insured is likely to meet the requirements for claims assistance. Usually, it is clear that the insured qualifies for benefits under the policy. Still, it is not uncommon for an individual or family member to misunderstand the terms of the policy and call the Claims Department seeking assistance for a benefit or situation that the policy was not written to cover.

Once it is determined that the insured may qualify for benefits, the claims personnel generally order a face-to-face assessment of the insured. This is usually conducted by a registered nurse, but may be completed by a physical or occupational therapist, depending on the reason for accessing benefits. Usually, these are completed in the insured's place of residence within 24 to 48 hours of the initial call.

Face-to-face benefit eligibility assessments are conducted to help the insurer understand the medical, physical or cognitive status and limitations of the insured. A strong assessment will include the assessor's observations and insights, to help the insurer better understand the needs of the insured.

For example: *William Dawes Insurance Company sends a nurse to conduct an assessment on 87-year-old Alice Welch. Alice needs assistance with two ADLs — bathing and dressing. During the assessment, the nurse observes that while Ms. Welch appears steady, she has great difficulty raising her leg to step over the tub enclosure and bending to put on her shoes and stockings. This difficulty is exacerbated by her weight and arthritic hip. She appears independent in all other activities of daily living. The nurse assessor also notes that the insured has two children and three grandchildren living nearby.*

Knowing this, the insurer can develop a plan of care based on Ms. Welch's actual care needs. The plan of care is designed to help Ms. Welch maintain as much independence as possible. Under this plan of care, services initially start as bathing and dressing visits three times per week for two hours each. The insured's family wishes to help her dress on the remaining days, but they are unskilled in helping an elderly woman bathe.

Soon, thanks to home modifications paid for under the Alternative Plan of Care provision, assistive devices to aid in getting dressed, and payments by the insurer to provide family members with caregiver training, Ms. Welch is able to care for herself with minimal assistance from family members.

Some might argue that the insurer only paid for all of this training and services to avoid paying an extended claim. Whereas that would certainly be an important factor, few could argue about the value to the insured of regaining, or enhancing her sense of independence.

Insurers may also write for copies of medical records to better understand the needs and limitations of an individual applying for benefits. It is especially helpful when the insurer obtains copies of hospital discharge notes for claims following hospitalization.

<u>Evaluating Ongoing Eligibility</u>

As previously stated, the Long Term Care claim is rarely a simple approve or disapprove as with a life, auto, or medical claim. Unlike most other insurance products, the claims staff must develop an ongoing relationship with the insured. In addition to determining if the insured qualifies for benefits, they must also determine how much care is needed and for how long.

The degree of investigation may vary considerably, based on the disability the insured is suffering from and the type of care being provided. Many insurers have benchmarking standards for some of the more common conditions, but most also recognize that no two individuals are the same. The degree of dependency for a condition may vary considerably, depending on the age of the claimant and the impact of other medical conditions on the individual.

Claims managers often base their investigations and the type of requirements that they obtain by categorizing the claim as acute, chronic or cognitive. Additionally, the degree of active claims management should be expected to vary by claim type.

Acute: These claims are those that would not be expected to last more than 180 days and from which the insured would be expected to continually improve and eventually recover. Some examples of acute claims would be knee replacements and bypass surgery.

These claimants generally require more intensive claims management in order to ensure that the claimant utilize all available resources to fully recover.

Chronic: Some individuals suffer from chronic debilitating disorders such as severe rheumatoid arthritis or Parkinson's Disease. These individuals would be expected to continue on claim for an extended period, and in many cases, to worsen as time goes on.

These claimants require significant upfront management to help guide them towards the most appropriate care. However, the need for active management of the claim diminishes over time.

Cognitive: A decline in cognitive function may also eventually lead to the need for Long Term Care benefits. Cognitive decline may be slowly or rapidly progressive, or may be the result of an acute event such as a stroke. Individuals generally present for claim once their cognitive function has declined to the point where the individual would be a danger to themselves or others unless constantly supervised.

A cognitive claim requires substantial management up-front. The claims manager works closely with family members and community resources to enable the policyholder to age in their home as long as possible. Active claims management would diminish once the claimant's status has been confirmed, and a care routine is established.

In addition to determining if the claim is acute, chronic, or cognitive, the claims staff may vary their investigation depending on whether the care is being provided in a home or community setting, an assisted living facility or in a nursing home.

As with any insurance product, most individuals who file Long Term Care claims have a legitimate need. Each type of care is subject to misuse and abuse if not properly monitored. One duty of the claims staff is to limit the number of individuals who would abuse the insurance. This helps insurers focus their resources on those who most need it and limits the need for future rate increases.

Home and Community Care: This feature is perhaps the most attractive of a Long Term Care policy because it enables the individual to remain in their own home with limited outside support. Those who need assistance with their ADLs are far more likely to file a home care claim than to enter a confined care facility. Some of the features of home and community care, however, better lend themselves to misuse. Companion care, personal care and homemaker benefits are actually attractive to many lonely, isolated seniors. Although few would be inclined to initiate a false claim simply to access these benefits, many would hesitate to relinquish them once they have begun receiving them.

Additionally, many in the field consider home and community benefits to be more susceptible to provider fraud and abuse than other Long Term Care services.

This increased potential for malingering, abuse, and provider fraud necessitate greater ongoing scrutiny of the insured's ADL limitations and needs. Follow-up telephone assessments, as well as announced and unannounced face-to-face assessments would be more common for home and community benefits, especially in the early months of a claim.

Assisted Living Facilities: Most contracts today cover care in an assisted living facility or ALF. ALFs are fairly new in our society and have just begun to proliferate in the senior market over the past decade. Given the minimal experience data available for ALF use, these represent the great unknown for LTC claims management.

Assisted living facilities are far more attractive than nursing home confinements for most individuals, since these facilities offer a greater degree of independence. Also, they allow an ADL impaired individual to continue to live with their spouse rather than being separated in a nursing home environment.

These factors combine to necessitate the need for early, active intervention. The insurer's claims staff must both confirm the need for benefits and work to help the individual recover as quickly as possible while they are still cooperative. The general belief within the insurance community is that once an individual or couple has sold their home or apartment, they would be less motivated to recover completely as they may then be required to establish new living arrangements.

Nursing Homes: Among the common types of care available under the provisions of a Long Term Care policy, nursing home claims are perhaps the simplest to manage. Whereas our society has seen noticeable improvements in the quality of the facilities, staff and care, the stigma and total surrender of independence associated with nursing home admissions help *to ensure that only those truly in need admit themselves.*

Confirming claims eligibility is fairly easy with most nursing homes, because they keep detailed care records on each patient. The difficulty associated with managing a claim for nursing home coverage is in trying to help the claimant avoid admission or limiting it to a very short stay.

Although there are certainly some individuals for whom nursing home care is the best option, insurers consider helping most claimants avoid a nursing home confinement as a "win/win" strategy. The dollar savings are an obvious win for the insurer, and helping an elderly individual maintain a sense of control and independence in their lives is considered a significant "win" for the claimant as well.

It is important to recognize that no two claims will be treated identically. A good insurer will recognize the unique needs of the insured at claim time and will work hard to ensure that they are providing sufficient care to help the individual maintain the highest degree of independence possible. It is also helpful to realize that the financial savings associated with a decreased cost of care not only benefit the insurer, but may very well benefit all insureds in the long run by minimizing the need for rate increases.

Contestability & Fraud

This text previously discussed the fundamental principle of insurance. That is, that insurance is purchased to protect an individual from an unforeseen risk. Unfortunately, there are a minority of individuals who don't purchase insurance products for an unforeseen financial risk, but because they are aware of a particular risk that they do not wish to pay for themselves.

Insurance products were not designed or priced for those who would deliberately hide their medical or cognitive conditions to make others pay their bills. Underwriting is the first line of defense against these individuals. Claims investigation, however, is the last line of defense. Therefore, policies generally have protective contestability and fraud clauses, which are designed to help insurers protect themselves from dishonest individuals.

The contestability provision is a standard feature of almost all insurance policies. This provision usually indicates that the insurer made their decision to issue coverage based upon the answers and statements provided on the application for insurance. If, for some reason, the information that the insurer relied upon was incorrect, they reserve the right to reform (change) or rescind (take back) the policy.

This clause varies by state, but generally allows the insurer 24 months from the policy issue date to take any adverse action based on the statements provided in the application. Some states allow the insurer to reform or rescind for any material misrepresentation within 24 months. Others allow only six months for any material misrepresentation, but extend that to 24 months if the information omitted from the application is directly related to the cause of claim.

<u>For example:</u> 72-year-old Florence Curran applied for Long Term Care insurance on January 9[th,] 2003. The application indicated that she had seen Dr. Smith four months prior for her annual checkup and that "everything was OK". All other application questions were answered "no" and the policy was issued as applied for. Eight months later Ms. Curran submitted a claim due to ADL limitations caused by a stroke that had occurred on August 12th, 2003.

While investigating the claim, the insurer learned that Ms. Curran had been treated for severe osteoporosis for the past four years and had incorrectly answered several questions on the application. Had the insurer known of Ms. Curran's history of osteoporosis at the time of underwriting, they would not have issued a policy.

If she lived in a state that allowed for a 24-month contestability for any cause, the company would be able to deny the claim and terminate the policy as of the date of its inception. The philosophy of this clause is that the insurer entered into a contract with Ms. Curran based on false information. Therefore, since disclosure of that information would have led to a decline by the underwriters, no condition should be covered.

Had she been a resident of a state that limited the ability to contest to six months for any reason, or 24 months only if related to the cause of claim, the policy would be allowed to stay in force. If, on the other hand, the claim were for an osteoporosis-related fracture, the company would be able to take action for up to 24 months.

The scenarios above outline what the company has the right to do in the event of a contestable claim. Each insurer sets their own standards of enforcement based heavily upon corporate philosophy, the strength of the case and their internal legal advice. Fortunately, most insurers tend to err on the side of caution rather than mistakenly rescind a policy from a client.

The fraud provision of a contract is similar to the contestability clause, but differs in two important ways. It provides the insurer with a greater advantage in that there is no established time frame limiting the company from taking legal action. On the other hand, the burden of proof is considerably greater because the insurer is usually required to prove that there was "intent" to defraud the company. The case above may imply that Ms. Curran misled the insurer, but would most likely not pass the test for intending to defraud the insurer.

Fraud cases are usually more obvious once they come to light.

For example: 67-year-old Chuck Tomeselli applied for a Long Term Care policy only two weeks after being diagnosed with Parkinson's Disease. Like most cases of Parkinson's Disease, it was only diagnosed after months of numerous tests and doctor visits. When he applied for coverage, he did not disclose the diagnosis, the tests or the names of any of the physicians consulted.

Four years later, Mr. Tomeselli's Parkinson's had progressed to the point where he could no longer perform all of his Activities of Daily Living, and he filed a claim against his LTC policy.

In this scenario, the insurer would have a reasonable argument for fraud and might deny the claim. The insurer could argue that it is unlikely that Mr. Tomeselli simply "forgot" to tell them about the Parkinson's, since he had been undergoing an intensive workup for months and had just been diagnosed weeks before filling out the application. They could argue that, at that point in time, scarcely an hour would go by without Mr. Tomeselli thinking about how the disease might impact his future.

Furthermore, the insurer could argue, Mr. Tomeselli answered "no" to several application questions, including a direct Parkinson's Disease question, one that asked for the names of all doctors consulted within the last six months, another asking if any special test had been performed, and a fourth question requesting the names and dosages of all current prescription medications.

This claim might well satisfy the standards for denial based on fraud. Even with the policy well beyond the 24-month contestable period, the insurer could determine that it is appropriate to deny the claim and rescind the insurance.

Rating Agencies

*"It's hard to make predictions,
especially about the future"*

Yogi Bera

When the consumer purchases an insurance product, he or she gets nothing tangible in return. Unlike a new home, automobile, or pair of shoes, the paper policy that is delivered to the insured generally has no extrinsic value. The policy is not something that the insured can resell to another individual in need of a Long Term Care policy.

An insurance policy is often the beginning of a long relationship between the insured and insurer. Few purchasers of shoes are concerned with the financial strength or solvency of the manufacturer. Once the consumer walks out of the store, it doesn't matter if the factory makes another million pairs or closes their doors. An insurance product, on the other hand, represents a promise — a promise that the insurer will pay all appropriate claims. Most important, the policy is a promise to be there when the insured needs them most. This may be next year or in 50 years. Without a belief in that promise, the insurance industry could not survive.

Understanding the financial strength and stability of an insurer is not easy. Few consumers have the time or resources to investigate each insurer they are considering. Instead, consumers have learned to rely on a handful of rating agencies to assist them with understanding the risk of purchasing a policy from one company rather than another.

Today, there are numerous rating agencies for insurance and financial products. The tables that follow show two of the more highly respected and most frequently cited ones. These agencies are commonly referenced in discussions about the financial strength and solvency of an insurer.

A.M. Best has developed a rating scale designed to provide an opinion of the financial strength of an insurer as well as the insurer's ability to meet its ongoing obligations to its policyholders. A.M. Best bases its findings on data provided by the insurer as well as on independent research. Even though these ratings are intended to help consumers and investors better understand the strength of the insurer, they should not be interpreted as a guarantee of any kind.

Rating	***Interpretation***
A++ and A+	*Superior:* Assigned to companies that are considered to have a superior ability to meet their ongoing obligations to policyholders.
A and A-	*Excellent:* Assigned to companies that are considered to have an excellent ability to meet their ongoing obligations to policyholders.
B++ and B+	*Very Good:* Assigned to companies that are considered to have a good ability to meet their ongoing obligations to policyholders.

B and B-   *Fair:* Assigned to companies that are considered to have a fair ability to meet their current obligations to policyholders, but are financially vulnerable to adverse changes in underwriting and economic conditions.

C++ and C+   *Marginal:* Assigned to companies that are considered to have a marginal ability to meet their current obligations to policyholders, but are financially vulnerable to adverse changes in underwriting and economic conditions.

C and C-   *Weak:* Assigned to companies that are considered to have a weak ability to meet their current obligations to policyholders, but are financially very vulnerable to adverse changes in underwriting and economic conditions.

D   *Poor:* Assigned to companies that may not have an ability to meet their current obligations to policyholders and are financially extremely vulnerable to adverse changes in underwriting and economic conditions.

E   *Under Regulatory Supervision:* Assigned to companies that have been placed by an insurance regulatory authority under a significant form of supervision, control or restraint, whereby they are no longer allowed to conduct normal ongoing insurance operations. This would include conservatorship or rehabilitation, but does not include liquidation. It may also be assigned to companies issued cease and desist orders by regulators outside their home state or country.

F   *In Liquidation:* Assigned to companies that have been placed under an order of liquidation by a court of law or whose owners have voluntarily agreed to liquidate the company. Note: Companies that voluntarily liquidate or dissolve their charters are generally not insolvent.

S   *Rating Suspended:* Assigned to rated companies that have experienced sudden and significant events affecting their balance sheet strength or operating performance whose rating implications cannot be evaluated due to a lack of timely or adequate information.

Standard & Poor's is another respected rating agency that helps to provide insight into an insurer's ability to pay its future claims according to the terms of the policies. Ratings are based on information furnished by the insurance companies as well as other sources that Standard & Poor's deems reliable.

Rating   *Interpretation*

AAA   *Extremely strong* financial security characteristics.

AA   *Very strong* financial security characteristics.

A   *Strong* financial security characteristics, but somewhat more likely to be affected by adverse business conditions than are insurers with higher ratings.

BBB   *Good* financial security characteristics, but is more likely to be affected by adverse business conditions than are higher rated insurers.

BB   *Marginal* financial security characteristics. Positive attributes exist, but adverse business conditions could lead to insufficient ability to meet financial commitments.

B   *Weak* financial security characteristics. Adverse business conditions will likely impair its ability to meet financial commitments.

CCC   *Very weak* financial security characteristics, and is dependent on favorable business conditions to meet financial commitments.

C   *Extremely weak* financial security characteristics and is likely not to meet some of its financial commitments.

R   *Under regulatory supervision* owing to its financial condition. Regulators may have the power to favor one class of obligation over another.

Consumers will benefit from understanding the financial ratings of a particular insurer before purchasing an insurance policy. The ratings are based largely on information that the insurer provides to the rating agency. No rating should be viewed as a guarantee of future financial strength or willingness to pay, but merely as one indicator of the insurers likely ability to pay future claim obligations.

The consumer must also understand that ratings may change over time. Rating agencies frequently meet with insurers to review and reanalyze their ratings. Ratings may increase or decrease over time based on a number of factors ranging from the amount of surplus capital available, to the insurers mix of business, and even to outside economic conditions, legislation, and the current legal environment.

Choosing a Long Term Care Policy

*"Never put off until tomorrow what you can do
the day after tomorrow"*

Mark Twain

The best plan for coping with the financial needs of a family member in a nursing home or in need of home care will differ from family to family. Competent professionals, such as elder law attorneys, can help a family choose the best way to prepare for this situation.

This section features a worksheet to help the consumer determine if the purchase of a Long Term Care policy makes sense for his or her personal situation. The worksheet will help to identify which aspects of an LTC policy are most important to each individual consumer. If possible, the consumer should attempt to determine price ranges for each factor to determine if the value of a particular benefit provision is worth the extra premium.

Choosing which features to purchase in an LTC policy is much like any other large purchase. The buyer must consider a cost-benefit analysis of the policy. Affordability issues must be weighed carefully. Some options might need to be eliminated in order to ensure affordability. Because of this, the buyer may want to make extra copies of the following worksheet in order to recalculate the cost-benefits of policy provisions until the right mix of affordability and benefits is determined.

Long Term Care Worksheet

- Reason for considering purchase of long term care:
  - ❑ Estate protection
  - ❑ To afford care that will help me age in place
  - ❑ Other _____

- Total assets: $ _____

- Affordability Cap: (total assets X 3%):_____

- Total assets excluding primary residence, automobile, and burial funds: $ _____

- Annual Income:
  - ❑ Single: _____
  - ❑ Joint: _____

- Affordability Cap: (total income X 7%): _____

- Indicate nearby family members and friends who might be called on to assist you in the absence of long term care insurance:
  - ❑ Spouse: _____
  - ❑ Siblings: _____
  - ❑ Children: _____
  - ❑ Grandchildren: _____
  - ❑ Other: _____

- Indicate preference of tax-qualified or non-qualified:
  - ❑ Tax qualified
  - ❑ Non tax-qualified
  - Reason for preference: _____
  _____

- Indicate preference for reimbursement or indemnity:
  - ❑ Reimbursement
  - ❑ Indemnity
  - Reason for preference: _____
  _____

- Indicate preference for types of care provided:
  - ❑ Facility care only
  - ❑ Home care only
  - ❑ Comprehensive (facility & home care)
  - Reason for preference: _____
  _____

- Indicate optional benefits desired as well as reasons for choosing the benefit:
  - ❑ Waiver of Premium
    Reason: _____

  - ❑ Waiver of Premium upon Death of Spouse
    Reason: _____

  - ❑ Waiver of Premium if spouse is on Claim
    Reason: _____

  - ❑ Inflation protection (simple)
    Reason: _____

❑ Inflation protection (compound)
Reason: _____

❑ Guaranteed purchase option
Reason: _____

❑ Return of Premium
Reason: _____

❑ Return of Premium upon Death
Reason: _____

❑ Contingent Benefit
Reason: _____

❑ Non Forfeiture Benefit
Reason: _____

❑ Other: _____
Reason: _____

- Indicate the daily benefit amount desired:
  ❑ Facility care daily amount $ _____
  ❑ Home and community care
  daily amount $ _____
  How were these amounts determined?: _____
  _____

- Indicate elimination period desired:
  ❑ 0 Days   ❑ 20/30 Days
  ❑ 60 Days   ❑ 90/100 Days
  Reason for preference: _____
  _____

- Indicate preference of service day or calendar day elimination period:
  ❑ Service Days
  ❑ Calendar Days
  Reason for preference: _____
  _____

- Indicate benefit period desired:
  ❑ 2 years   ❑ 3 years
  ❑ 4 years   ❑ 5 years
  ❑ Lifetime / Unlimited
  Reason for preference: _____
  _____

- Indicate premium payment plan desired:
  ❑ Pay premiums for life of policy
  ❑ Pay premiums for 10 years
  ❑ Pay premiums until age 65
  ❑ Single premium payment
  Reason for preference: _____
  _____

- Indicate importance of insurance company ratings
  ❑ Very important
  ❑ Somewhat important
  ❑ Not too important
  ❑ Doesn't matter

__Conclusion__

*"Beginnings and endings represent the same
event from a different point of view"*

Albert Emerson Unaterra

This book demonstrates the complexity of Long
Term Care insurance. Unlike many other types of
insurance, there are numerous variables and options.
The consumer must decide between reimbursement
and indemnity, tax-qualified and non tax-qualified.
Decisions must be made regarding elimination
periods, benefit periods, and the amount of daily
benefit to purchase.

Insurers package their Long Term Care products in
ways that make it difficult to compare. Underwriting
criteria, requirements, and decisions may vary
significantly from one company to another. All of
these factors make it nearly impossible to measure
"apples to apples".

Consumers should take the time to research their
options. Long Term Care is an expensive purchase.
A 65 year old could easily pay upwards of $2,000 per
year in premium. Given an average remaining life
expectancy of eighteen years, that 65 year old could
pay $36,000 or more for this protection, and that's
assuming no rate increases. That significant of an
investment is well worth the time and energy required
to do some research.

Additionally, individual needs vary considerably. Some may purchase Long Term Care insurance for estate protection, while others purchase it to ensure that they will have choices in quality care should they ever find themselves impaired. Some consumers have strong support networks of friends and families, while others have few family members or other support networks nearby.

Whereas many qualify for Long Term Care insurance, even some with significant medical history, some will find themselves uninsurable. Long Term Care insurance is generally available up to age 85, and sometimes beyond, but premiums rise considerably with age as does the risk of becoming uninsurable.

Knowledge of the various product offerings will enable the consumer to make more educated choices. Understanding what to expect during the underwriting and claims process will make both easier to understand and often help to expedite a final decision.

This book is intended to be a resource to the consumer as they travel through the purchasing, underwriting, and possibly even the claims processes. With a small investment of time, a bit of research, and a fundamental knowledge of Long Term Care insurance, the reader will be far better prepared for the decisions that lie ahead.

<u>Glossary</u>

Activities of Daily Living: Bathing, Continence, Dressing, Eating, Toileting, and Transferring

ADL: Activities of Daily Living

Alternative Plan of Care: Care that is not specifically included in the policy which may be approved by the insurance company

Assisted Living Facility: Continuous care facilities that house both independent and ADL dependent individuals

Baby Boomer: Those born from 1946-1964

Benefit Period: The maximum period of time for which benefits will be paid

Centenarian: Those who have reached the age of 100 or greater

Certification (90 day): HIPAA requirement that care must be expected to last at least 90 days in order for benefits to be paid

Claims Management: The process of determining benefit eligibility and determining appropriate levels of care

Cognitive Impairment: Diminished cognitive ability that places the individual at risk to themselves or others

Community Care: Care that is provided in one's home or other non-facility setting

Comprehensive Policies: Includes both community and facility care

Contestability: The provision in a policy that permits the insurer to deny a claim based on omissions or misstatements on the application

Custodial Care: Care that is not medical, but palliative, in nature

Daily Benefit: The dollars available for one day of care

Deductible: Elimination period

Elimination Period: The period of care that must be paid for by the insured before benefits become payable

English Poor Laws of 1601: The first codification if Western ideals of societal responsibility for the poor

Fraud: The policy provision that permits the insurer to deny a claim based on deliberate misrepresentation

Guaranteed Renewable: The provision that prohibits the insurer from canceling coverage, but allows for rate increases subject to state approval

Health Insurance Portability and Accountability Act: Legislation that established standardized definitions and favorable tax treatment for some Long Term Care policies

HIPAA: Health Insurance Portability and Accountability Act

Home Health Care: Care provided in one's home

IADL: Instrumental Activities of Daily Living

Indemnity Policy: One that pays a predetermined benefit regardless of the actual cost of care

Instrumental Activities of Daily Living: Transport, Shopping, Housework, Meal Preparation, Laundry, Finances, Taking Medication, and Using the Telephone

Institutional Care: Confined care such as a nursing home or hospice facility

Long Term Care Insurance: Insurance that provides assistance for those with ADL limitations

LTC: Long Term Care

Medicaid: Joint federal and state welfare program that provides some long term care protection for the poor

Medical Necessity: The benefit trigger that permits a licensed health care professional to determine if a policy holder should receive benefits

Medicare: Joint federal and state insurance program that provides limited home health care for senior citizens

Non Tax Qualified: Policies not covered under HIPAA for favorable tax treatment

Nursing Home: Live-in Facilities designed primarily to provide skilled nursing care

Plan of Care: Claim document outlining the type, amount, and duration of care needed

Pool of Money: Benefit period based on a dollar amount rather than a time period

Rating Agencies: Organizations that provide evaluations of an insurers ability to meet their financial obligations

<u>Notes</u>

<u>Notes</u>

Notes

Notes

Printed in the United States
38939LVS00005BB/64

9 781414 038674